PIANO SOLO
SELECTIONS FROM THE ORIGINAL MOTION PICTURE SOUNDTRACK

STAR WARS®: EPISODE II
ATTACK OF THE CLONES®

PROJECT MANAGER: CAROL CUELLAR
ART LAYOUT: KEN REHM

CONTENTS

ACROSS THE STARS
(Love Theme From
Star Wars®: Episode II) . . . 9

THE ARENA . . . 26

DUEL OF THE FATES
(Featured Theme in "Return to Tatooine"). . . 14

IMPERIAL MARCH
(Featured Theme in
"Confrontation With Count Dooku and Finale"). . . 30

MAY THE FORCE BE WITH YOU
(Featured Theme in "Return to Tatooine"). . . 32

THE MEADOW PICNIC. . . 23

STAR WARS (Main Title). . . 34

ACROSS THE STARS
(LOVE THEME FROM *STAR WARS: EPISODE II*)

Music by
JOHN WILLIAMS

Moderately slow & gently (♩ = 76)

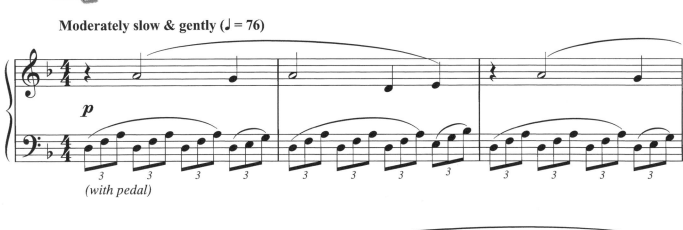

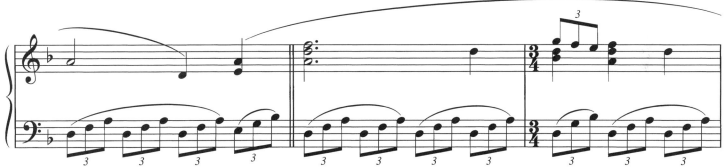

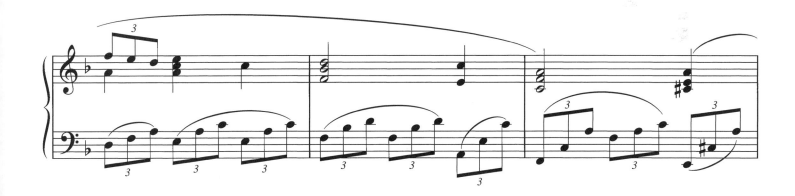

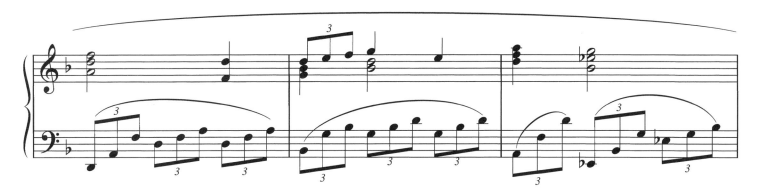

Across the Stars - 5 - 1
0683B

Appassionato

DUEL OF THE FATES

Music by
JOHN WILLIAMS

Maestoso, with great force

Kor - ah,_____ Mah - tah._____ Kor - ah,_____ Rah-tah - mah.___

Allegro ♩ = 152

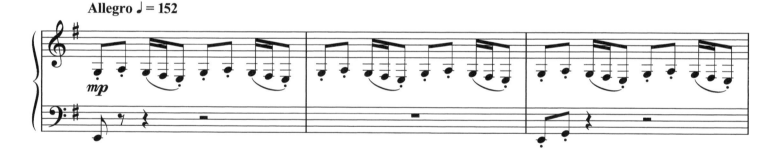

Duel of the Fates - 9 - 1
0683B

Yood - hah,

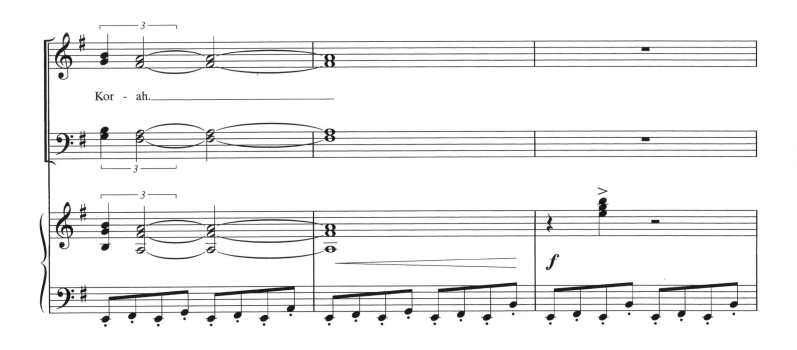

Kor - ah.

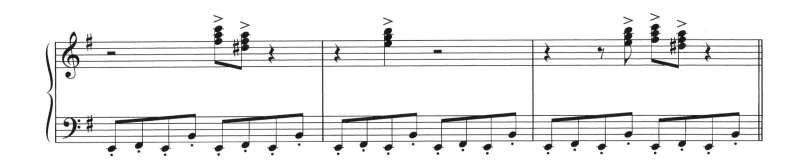

Kor - ah,_____ Syahd - ho._____

Rah - tah - mah,_____

Daan - yah._____ Kor - ah,_____

Kor - ah,_____ Daan - yah.

Kor - ah,_____ Rah - tah - mah.

Duel of the Fates - 9 - 8
0683B

THE MEADOW PICNIC

Music by
JOHN WILLIAMS

The Meadow Picnic - 3 - 1
0683B

24

THE ARENA

Music by
JOHN WILLIAMS

Maestoso (♩ = 88)

The Arena - 4 - 1
0683B

Slightly faster

THE IMPERIAL MARCH
(DARTH VADER'S THEME)

Music by
JOHN WILLIAMS

In march style

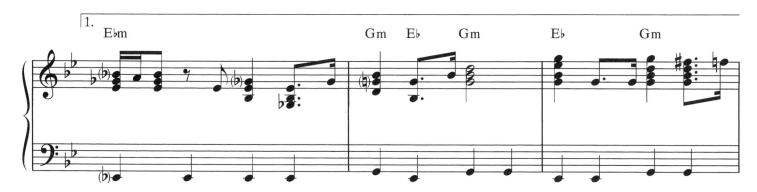

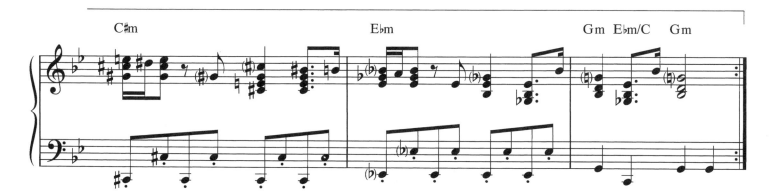

The Imperial March - 2 - 1
0683B

MAY THE FORCE BE WITH YOU

Music by
JOHN WILLIAMS

May the Force Be With You - 2 - 2
0683B

STAR WARS
(MAIN TITLE)

Music by
JOHN WILLIAMS

March (Majestic)

Star Wars - 2 - 1
0683B